Listening and Speaking Skills for Leaders

SpeechSHARK

Participant Handbook

AF438454

LAWRENCEVILLE | ALPHARETTA-NORTH FULTON

www.innovativeinkpublishing.com
Send all inquiries to:
4050 Westmark Drive
Dubuque, IA 52004-1840

Copyright © 2025 Penny Joyner Waddell

ISBN: 979-8-3851-7254-2

A Note from the Author

Workshop Objectives

Participant Handbooks are designed to fully include all seminar content along with a copy of PowerPoint slides and class notes. Pertinent information is included, so students have access to materials that might not be included during shorter sessions. This allows for self-study and reflection following the seminar. To make best use of this material, plan to participate in each section marked as a **Course Activity**. Read each question, consider the points, and answer them honestly. Fill in the blanks positioned throughout the book and internalize how these activities will help improve your skills.

Facilitators do not have a magic wand to wave over participants and automatically transfer skills shared in a professional development session. Instead, it takes commitment and determination for the participant to learn skills and practice them repeatedly until the new skill becomes a new habit.

Best regards as you complete this seminar to better understand the nuances surrounding Listening and Speaking for Leaders and their impact upon personal and professional development.

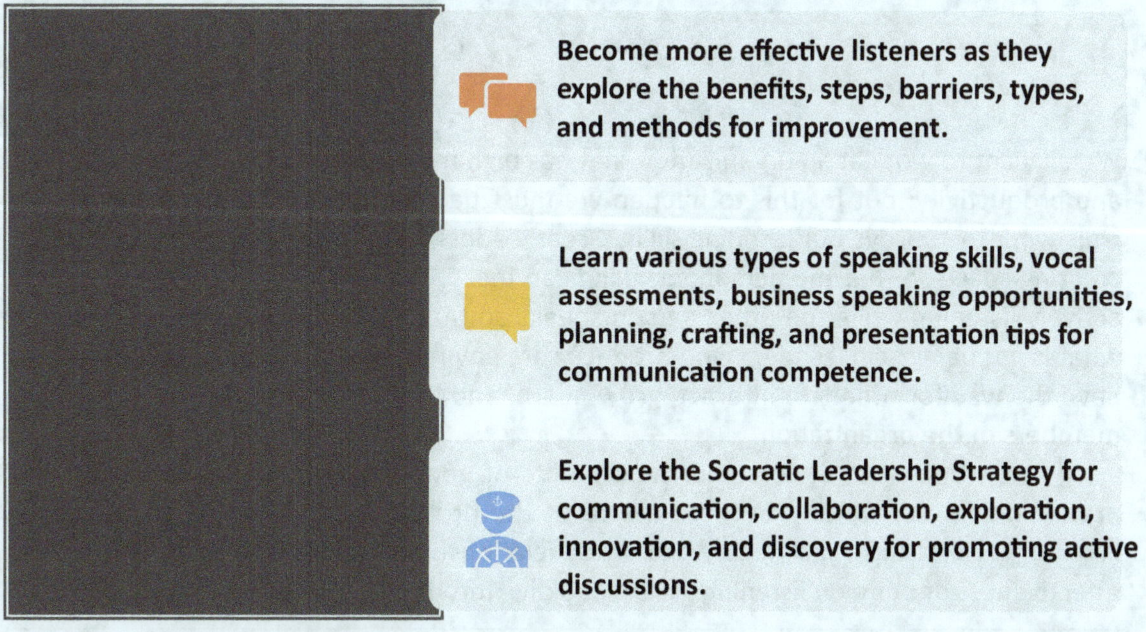

Misunderstandings and miscommunications happen often and it is not surprising that organizations and businesses include *Listening and Speaking* professional development opportunities to improve communication skill deficiencies. *Active Listening Statistics: Insights and Trends 2025*, reports that "most people spend 45% of their communication time listening" (Jobera), yet ineffective communication skills are blamed for workplace mistakes that costs organizations millions of dollars each year. If you have ever doubted the importance of listening, then you might be interested to know that _______________ ____________________________ is **good for business** as the graphic below demonstrates:

We all want to work at an organization that has high morale, increased job commitment, and productivity, but for this to happen we must become more effective listeners and truly *want* to improve our listening skills. Great leaders understand that listening is about creating space so that the person speaking can feel ___________________. It means actively listening while the other person speaks so that we hear what is being said and what is *not* being said. Leaders who produce safe environments for candid conversations pave the way for others to interact, grow, learn, and think of themselves as _________ members of the organization.

As we seek to understand the benefits of good listening for our personal and professional lives, we also become aware of the problems that arise when we fail at listening. Friendships, marriages, and work relationships are made and broken by the effectiveness of our own listening skills. Let's dive into this a bit deeper.

Listening lays the foundation needed for a clear *understanding* of the message.
- **Listen.** Listen more and talk less.
- **Listen.** Encourage the speaker to keep talking by using _________________ nods, eye contact, or gestures.
- **Listen.** Resist the urge to ______________ right away.
- **Listen.** Allow the speaker to finish what they are saying.
- **Listen.** Allow the speaker to feel heard.

Understanding fosters an appropriate *response*.
- **Listen.** Determine if the speaker needs help or just needs to be heard.
- **Listen.** Respond with empathy, caring, and kindness.
- **Listen.** Show __________________ in speaker's ability.

An appropriate *response* creates *high-quality communication*.
- **Listen.** Model good listening skills so others will also be prompted to listen.
- **Listen.** Communication is a ____________________. It's not all about you.

High-quality communication promotes *organizational cooperation*.
- **Listen.** Foster a cooperative culture by ______________.
- **Listen.** Build relationships and influence performance.

Organizational cooperation improves *morale*.
- **Listen.** Create a workspace that __________________ others.
- **Listen.** Appreciate and reward positive movements toward performance.
- **Listen.** Reward high performers.
- **Listen.** Coach others toward excellence.

High morale increases *job commitment*.
- **Listen.** Encourage problem solving and creativity toward meeting needs.
- **Listen.** Create healthy, _____________ environments to reduce conflict.

Job commitment improves *productivity*.
- **Listen.** Provide training and development for the "whole" person.
- **Listen.** Empower others by setting goals, values, and challenges.
- **Listen.** Show confidence in others' ability to excel.

Listening, Understanding, Responding, Communicating, Cooperating, Building High Morale, Increasing Job Commitment, and Improving Productivity are

Good for Business

Leaders who listen:
- ✓ Know their staff members
- ✓ Easily identify emerging problems
- ✓ Discover relevant solutions
- ✓ Resolve problems before they escalate
- ✓ Avoid difficult conversations

Course Activity: Throughout the work-week, we spend hours of our working lives involved in listening-related activities. Indicate which of the following activities apply to you. Add other activities that are involved during your work day.

______ Assisting customers

______ Assisting co-workers

______ Attending meetings

______ Giving instructions

______ Receiving instructions

______ Managing others

______ Answering phone calls

______ Servicing others (individuals, groups, or departments)

______ Making decisions based on verbal information

______ Selling or marketing a product or service

______ Troubleshooting problems

______ Add other listening activities

Would you like to learn how to improve your listening skills?

Learn	Learn the benefits of effective listening
Follow	Follow the listening steps
Understand	Understand the difference between listening and hearing
Avoid	Avoid barriers to listening
Practice	Practice five types of listening
Respond	Respond appropriately for active listening

The Benefits of Effective Listening: Dr. Manny Steil, a leading listening researcher said, "With millions of workers in this country, a simple $10.00 mistake by each one as a result of poor listening skills adds up to billions of dollars in lost productivity per year." While listening is a common communication skill, it is not always a mastered skill. We spend more time listening than any other physical activity except for breathing, yet we only listen using a small fraction of our potential. We've discussed how effective listening skills are good for business, but they are also necessary for healthy relationships in our personal lives.

Effective listening skills help avoid more problems in the workplace and at home than any other skill. It is an incredibly powerful tool for success, but listening involves using more than just your ears. Sure, you need to use your ears to listen, but you also need your eyes, and an awareness of the situation, also known as your instincts.

Watch and Learn: When listening to a speaker, pay attention to everything you see: body movements, posture, gestures, eye contact, and object usage. _____________ sent nonverbally can often speak louder than the words being used.

Listen and Learn: The speaker's _____________________ (tone, volume, pitch, pace, rate, and color) will share whether the speaker is happy, sad, anxious, calm, frustrated, or contented.

Use Eye Contact: Connect with the speaker using good eye contact, but also be aware of the speaker's eye contact cues. Avoiding eye contact sends a message that you might not be hearing the entire story.

Match Cues to Meaning: We tend to believe what we see more than what we hear. Listen to the speaker's words, but be aware if the nonverbal cues do not match the speaker's message.

Consider the Message: Context means everything. Consider the situation in which the message is delivered. This helps as you match the nonverbal cues to the message and determine if the situation alters the intended meaning. Your ability to encode and decode messages is key to moving the conversation in a positive direction. Being sensitive to cultures that differ from our own will help us to be better listeners and communicators. Knowing whether to shake hands, bow, or nod can be the difference between closing a deal or closing a door.

ASK Questions: Did you know that **ASK is an acronym for Actively Seeking Knowledge?** It is good to ask questions, but only when the conversation begins to lull. When you see nonverbal signals that conflict with the message, ASK! You can rephrase the message, ask if you have the correct understanding, or ask for the speaker to elaborate. Avoid jumping in with your own thoughts or suggestions. Instead ASK open-ended questions and give space (time) for the speaker to elaborate, clarify, or complete the thought.

The more experience you have with identifying nonverbal messages, the easier it becomes to interpret cues being sent. People who are good listeners are also very good with understanding and interpreting nonverbal messages. Good listeners have better ________ ___________ than poor listeners and will usually read cues that others may miss.

Listen with your ears, eyes, and instincts to follow the listening steps:

Listening is an Important Communication Skill

Listening	Hearing
Activity	Process
Learned skill (taught and learned)	Response to stimuli and is involuntary
Requires the listener to be engaged, encode/decode, and respond	Passive and requires no action
Choice: requires focus and attention	If no hearing loss, hearing is continuous and ongoing
Message or content is consciously received and often gets a response	Sound is received but does not always elicit a response

Course Activity: Let's Talk About Listening vs. Hearing

What sounds are regularly heard in your workplace that requires no action or response?

What strategies do you use to avoid being distracted?

How could these sounds impact your listening skills?

How could these sounds create a problem in your workplace?

Do you want to become a better listener to improve your workplace and personal relationships? The key is getting along with others and learning about barriers that interfere. With so many barriers to listening, it is a wonder that we can communicate at all. The primary key to eliminating barriers is to be aware of them, recognize them as they happen, and take action steps toward eliminating the barriers and improving your listening skills. **Things we hear, things we see, things we do, things we know or don't know, and things we feel or perceive can distract us from listening to the speaker.**

Here are six common barriers to effective listening.

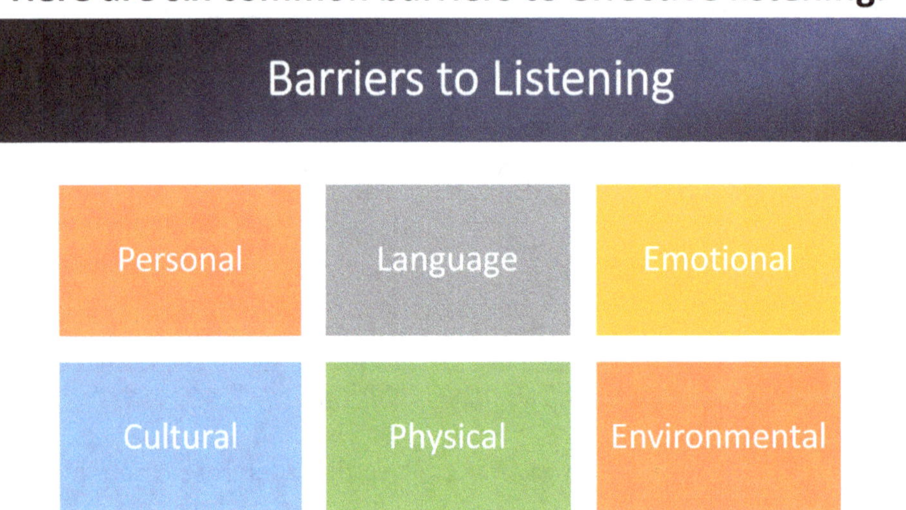

Personal: Many barriers can fit into this category. *Time* can be an issue if someone feels like they do not have time to really focus on what the speaker is needing to communicate. *Verbal* _____________________, such as questions, statements, or quick responses will cause listening to be challenged and focus broken. *Bias* or pre-conceived assumptions toward someone else or the topic can result in poor listening. _____________________, thinking about something or someone else, anxiety, thinking how to respond, or becoming bored and focusing on something else will become a barrier to listening. *Confusion of word meanings* can distract you from hearing the rest of the message as you wonder how the word is spelled or what the word means. *Relationship barriers* such as a lack of trust, unconscious bias, or lack of shared goals can cause the listener to withdraw attention to the speaker. This problem is usually related to a personal dynamic between yourself and the speaker. Building the relationship through seeking common goals will help align the conversation so that it is mutually beneficial to both parties.

Language: *Differences in languages* spoken between two people is a common obstacle for effective listening, especially when one person has a poor understanding of the language spoken. ________________ or accents may also cause barriers. The *tone, pace, or rate* of speech often causes a listening barrier since these carry a nonverbal element that does not match with words being spoken.

Emotional: *Positive or negative emotions* that deter effective listening include being overly *excited, angry, frustrated, or distracted*. These emotional factors make it difficult to focus on what is being said and serve as a negative barrier to listening. *Thoughts* while listening, such as thinking about a ________________ or *judging the speaker* can break our listening focus and lead to miscommunication and misunderstandings. *Grief* and our reactions to grief can be barriers as we consider what to say or how to respond to those who are grieving. ____________________________ may be a subtle barrier, but certainly creates the perfect storm for effective listening as our brains tend to focus on the stressful matter at hand instead of a message being delivered through a speaker.

Cultural: *Company cultures* show up in meetings as barriers to effective listening. This could involve a ____________________________ where members will not speak until the head supervisor has spoken. It could also involve action orientation where employeers are constantly rushing to the next action. In this case, it is important to use opportunities to slow down and listen. Other companies focus on the urgent without stopping to listen for the key issues that need to be addressed. Again, the best response is to slow down. Reflect on a path forward, and listen. *Differences* in generations, religious or political affilitations, social status, gender, customs, traditions, or ethnicies can also create barriers between the speaker and the listener.

Physical: *Noise, obstructions, distance, perceptions, moods*, and anything that blocks our ability to intentionally listen to what is being said is considered a physical barrier. Focusing too much on the speaker's ____________________, *filler words, movements, or language skills* can cause the listener to judge the speaker and quit listening to what is being said.

Environmental: Meeting in *overly populated spaces* can make conversations difficult from the speaker's perspective and also from the listener's perspective. If one or both parties are *tired, hungry, or ill*, a barrier can be present causing the message to be distorted or not completely heard. Technological barriers such as phones, email alerts, and other apps that "ping" often distract us from listening activities.

"The most important thing in communication
is hearing what isn't said."

~Peter Drucker, Author, Educator, and American Management Consultant

All barriers mentioned here, nonverbal and verbal signs, will usually indicate if someone is an ineffective listener. **Nonverbal cues** include the person doing other things while appearing to listen, such as reading, typing, sending texts or emails, yawning, drumming their fingers, checking their phone or watch, clearing off a desk, or any number of tasks. Other nonverbal signs may inclde the person's shoulders facing away from the speaker, poor eye contact, slouching in a chair, crossing arms over their chest, putting hands in their pockets, or appearing to "look through" the speaker instead of at the speaker. ____________________**cues,** such as interrupting, premature responses, nodding with no eye contact, or replying with a dismissve attitude, will indicate a poor listener. These frustrating barriers can be eliminated, but it takes commitment from the speaker and the listener to do their part. This means keeping the conversation on point and focusing on the task at hand.

Listening is not just about hearing the words. Use all of your ____________so that you hear the words, see the speaker's nonverbal cues that are being sent, and feel the atmosphere surrounding the speaker and the message. We often rely on our senses to determine the accuracy of what we perceive and how we process that information. As you check the accuracy of your perceptions, you can also determine if you are in step with the speaker while the message is being delivered. Listen with your ears, yes, but also with your senses and you will overcome barriers to listening.

What listening skills do you use most often?

Active Listening:

listening to understand and observing nonverbal cues to see if they match the speaker's message

Critical Listening:

resisting outside noise, distractions, personal feelings or perceptions of the speaker or the message

Empathetic Listening:

trying to see the speaker's point of view

Informative Listening:

making notes of main points, data, or issues

Appreciative Listening:

showing enjoyment of the speaker and content

Would you like to learn a few phrases and questions that will improve your Listening Skills? In this section you will see examples that will help clarify the true message, troubleshoot issues, learn details, expose challenges, and build conversations.

Statement: I ______________ what you are saying.

ASK: Can you tell me more?

Could you clarify what you mean by…?

Could you elaborate on that?

What do you think is the best solution?

How does that make you feel?

Statement: Thank you for sharing your ______________.

ASK: Can you provide an example?

How does this align with your overall goals?

How can we address this issue?

How do you see this playing out?

Statement: I appreciate your __________________ on this.

ASK: It sounds like you are saying…

Can you walk me through your process?

What steps can we take to improve this?

What support do you need to move forward?

Statement: That's a great ____________________!

ASK: How did you reach that conclusion?

What challenges do you foresee?

Could you elaborate?

Poor listening skills cost organizations billions of dollars each year, but it also holds a personal cost, too, as marriages, friendships, and workplace relationships are broken when there is a breakdown in communication. Become a better listener and you will become a more effective employee, a better marriage partner, and a more reliable friend.

Here are some practical ways to break bad listening habits:

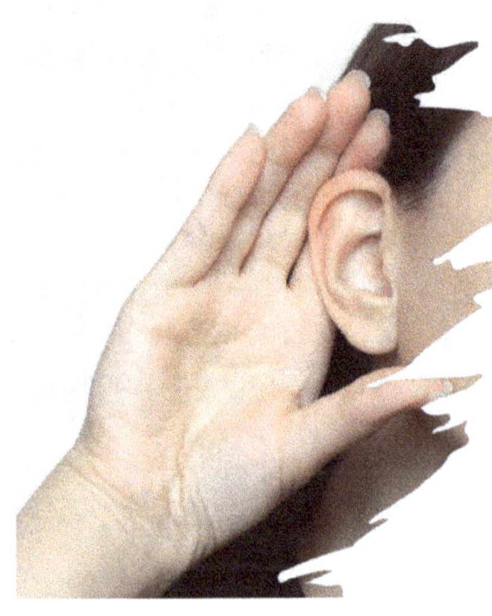

Course Activity: Let's talk about the one common characteristic in all bad listening habits. It's an atttude that "this conversation is all about me and what I want to say!"

How do bad listening habits affect relationships?

What effect does multi-tasking have on our listening skills?

Why does a "learning posture" help with listening skills?

What happens when you stop listening so that you can plan your response?

Why should you NOT say, "I know exactly how you feel!"?

What are open-ended questions?

True listening requires taking time to understand the speaker's perception.

The following lists twenty listening habits. On a scale of 1-5 with 1 as the best and 5 being the absolute worst, indicate the degree to which the habit describes you. Be honest with yourself. There is no grade for this, but recognizing our skill is the best way to make a change.

Rate	Characteristic
	I make regular eye contact with a speaker.
	I ask questions for clarification.
	I interrupt often.
	I show concern by ackowledging feelings.
	I jump to conclusions.
	I restate or paraphrase some of the speaker's words to show that I understand the message.
	I finish other people's sentences.
	I try to understand what someone is saying to me.
	I often change the subject of conversation.
	I can control my emotions when speaking with others.
	I use effective nonverbal cues such as eye contact, smiles or frowns, head nods, and gestures.
	I think about my reply while the other person is speaking.
	I stick to the subject.
	I pay attention and do not let my mind drift to something or someone else.
	I pay attention, but think of other things while the person is speaking.
	I make up my mind right away and before I have all of the information.
	I act responsibly on what I hear.
	I get impatient with a speaker that takes too much time.
	I become defensive when the speaker is argumentative or combative.
	I want the speaker to get to the point.

Now that we have a better understanding of our own listening skills, let's focus on our speaking skills. Afterall, good leaders need to be proficient at listening and speaking. Zig Ziglar said, *"You do not have to be great to start, but you have to start to be great."* So, let's get started!

Speakers have a responsibility to the audience. It is your job to know *who* will be in the audience and to plan a speech that provides the *content* they need or want to hear.

Speaking is a process in which speakers and listeners participate together. Content delivered from the speaker is received by the listener. In turn, the listener communicates through verbal or nonverbal cues to indicate an understanding or a lack thereof. In other words, this is a **transactional process** with participation between the sender (speaker) and the receiver (audience) that involves encoding and decoding for all participants. This explanation should help you to better understand the process.

_______________ is a process by which a person derives meaning and understanding. It may involve finding a common understanding to develop a deeper understanding of the point or the topic. Conducting research or speaking with someone who has experience about the topic helps the speaker to encode the message and develop a deeper understanding.

_______________ is a process by which we translate or interpret the content into meaning. This process can be altered depending upon noise in the environment.

_______________ can be defined as audible and nonaudible distractions in the speaking environment. Pre-conceived notions, opinions, ideas, objects, and sights can alter the feedback from the listener just as intensely as the sound of a lawn mower just outside the window.

_______________ can be verbal or nonverbal and it helps the speaker to know if the content has been delivered effectively and received.

From this diagram, you can see how the communication process works, but it also helps to visualize the importance of having effective listeners and effective speakers.

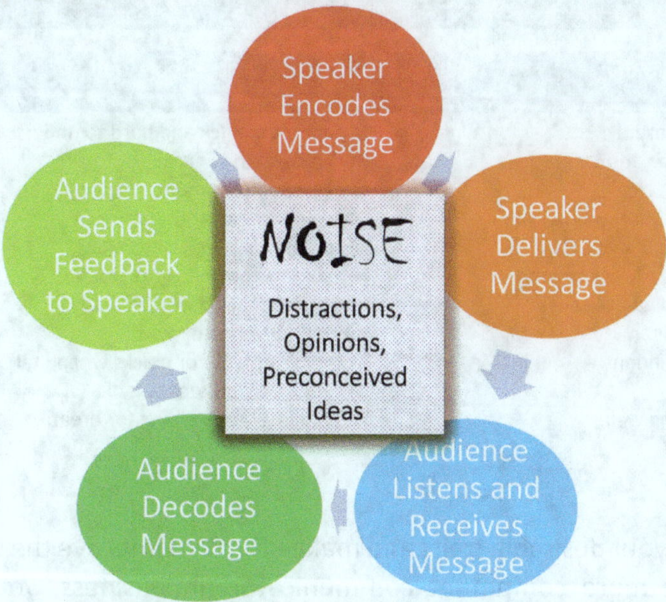

Do you need help finding your __________? If you have ever been asked what you think about an issue, or expected to speak to a group of people, you might have been stressed or possibly questioned your confidence with the answer. Speaking, sharing instructions, opinions, or facts are important for business. As a leader, you should work at becoming a competent speaker and using your voice to __________________ and bring positive change to the workforce. The more you advance in your company or organization, the more often you will be challenged with the prospect of speaking. Since this is going to be an ongoing reality in your life, take time now to find your voice and learn to speak eloquently.

Course Activity: Using your telephone, record your voice as you read the previous paragraph. Listen closely to the recording. Complete the **Vocal Self-Assessment** to determine the desirable and undesirable traits of your own voice.

What traits concern you most?
What action could you take to improve a negative trait?
What trait makes you feel more confident?

SpeechSH🦈RK. Vocal Self-Assessment

Desirable Traits	True/False	Undesirable Traits	True/False
My voice sounds pleasant.		My accent is thick and hard to understand.	
My voice has pitch variations.		My voice sounds nasal.	
My voice is light.		My voice sounds monotone.	
My voice has a pleasant rhythm.		My voice sounds throaty or raspy.	
My pitch is appealing.		My pitch is too high or too low.	
I articulate words clearly as I speak.		My voice is too soft or too loud.	
I sound like I am smiling as I speak.		I do not articulate words clearly.	
My vocal quality is clear.		I sound bored with myself.	
My voice sounds confident.		My voice squeaks or cracks when I talk.	
I like my voice.		My voice sounds weak.	
I control my breathing well.		I sound like I am gasping for breath.	

The goal is to keep your desirable traits and make efforts to improve the undesirable traits so that you are a more competent communicator. In business, you will find many opportunities for speaking. Here are a few examples:

- Introductions
- Intentional Greetings
- Impromptu Speaking
- Prepared Speaking
- Business Occasion Speeches
- Elevator Pitch
- Evaluations

While there are many different types of speeches, they all follow the same basic steps for planning a speech and a common design. Here are the 7 Steps:

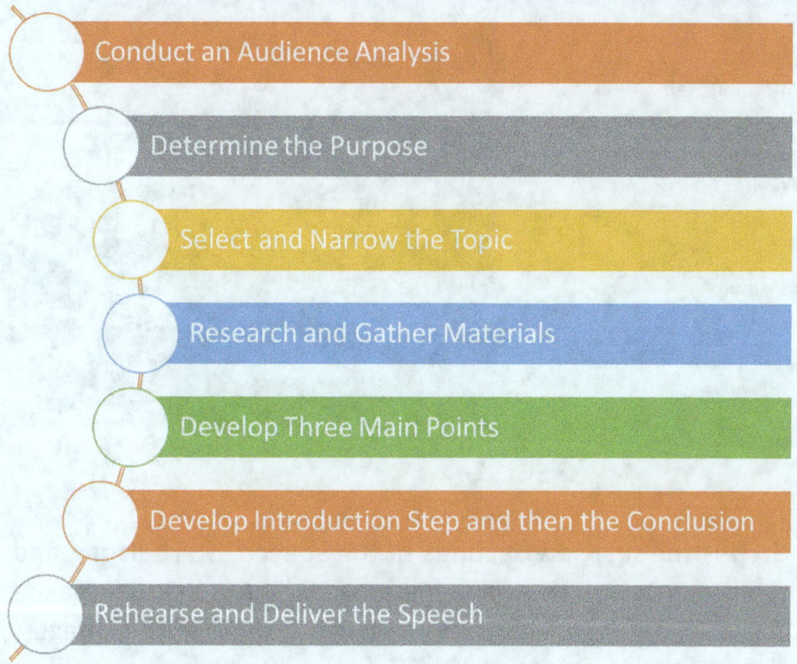

Knowing who is in your audience and determining the purpose (general and specific) of the speech will help you select and narrow the topic for the speech. Remember that the speech is designed for the audience. It's all about them and never about you. Once the topic has been chosen, it is time to conduct research and gather materials such as data, quotes, examples, or stories. Researched materials can help provide direction for your speech, but will most certainly help to strengthen your credibility as a speaker.

Each speech will have three main parts: Introduction, Body, and Conclusion.

Always construct the (1) ________ of the speech before you craft the (2) **Introduction** and the (3) **Conclusion**. Why? Because you should have a clear idea of the main point or points that will be covered before you introduce or conclude the speech. Take time to cover the main points, and include ______________ **Sentences** before and after each main point.

The **Introduction Step** should cover four important elements: Attention Step, Establish ___________________, Establish Relevance, and Preview Main Points.

I. **Introduction**
    A. Attention Step
    B. Establish Credibility
    C. Establish Relevance
    D. Preview Main Points

II. **Body**
    A. Cover Main Points
    B. Transitions

III. **Conclusion**
    A. Summary of Main Points
    B. End with a BANG!

The **Attention Step** is the first few seconds of the speech. Start strong and engage the audience by asking questions, showing empathy, telling a secret, making a startling statement, issuing warnings, sharing quotes, telling a story, inspiring imagery, or offering choices. In every case, the idea is to share your topic so the audience knows what you plan to cover during the speech. **Establish** ________________ to share your name, experience, and credibility for the topic. **Establishing Relevance** is designed so that your audience knows the topic and how the speech will benefit them. **Preview Main Points** for the audience to know exactly what you plan to cover. Now that you've set-up the speech, transition to the body of the speech where you will cover the topic, support points with relevant research, and provide content that is needed by the ________________. Transition sentences, also known as connectors, allow you to navigate easily from one main point to the next. It makes the move from one point to the next smooth.

The **Conclusion Step** is designed to include a Summary of Main Points and Final Comments. The **Summary of Main Points** will clearly restate each point that was covered during the speech and in the order they were covered. Depending upon the type speech you are presenting, the **Final Comments** which are intended to keep the audience thinking about your speech, could follow the same type plan as the introduction step. Just be sure to end your speech with a BANG and keep your audience wanting to hear more.

In your personal and professional life, you will have many opportunities to introduce yourself or others. Whether it is a planned or unplanned introduction, understanding these tips will help you present the introduction with ease. ______________________ speeches are informative in nature since they provide your audience with information about you or the person you are introducing. Usually this type of speech is not very long and will last about _________________ minutes. Since this is a short presentation, consider specific points to include, but without too much detail.

One safe strategy is to follow a chronological or time-ordered sequence to introduce yourself or someone else. The body of your speech can briefly cover (1) the past, (2) the present, and (3) the future. Consider the audience and the situation so you know what type and how much information you should cover.

Course Activity: Take five minutes to choose a person and interview them for this activity. Ask questions about about their past, present, and future as you write a few notes here. At the end of five minutes, be prepared to stand and introduce your classmate.

In business settings, you will often find the need for intentional greetings. These might happen first thing in the morning as you are walking into the building and you see someone who you need to meet with during that day or within a few days. This could also happen in the afternoon as you coincidently meet at the water fountain. When meetings of this type happen, it is helpful to always include an **intentional greeting**.

GOAL: Create high quality connections with short positive interactions for a positive outcome.

Greeting: Good morning, It is good to see you! How are you?

Define context: Share the purpose for the conversation in 3-5 words,

The goal is to create high quality connections with others to achieve a specific purpose.
Here is an example of an intentional greeting:
Hello, Sarah! I hope you are having a great Monday. Would you have a moment to tell me about the new position that just opened in the Human Resources department?

Course Activity: Let's Talk About It! What is another example that uses an intentional greeting strategy? Use this space to write the greeting:

Goal:

Greeting:

Context:

Impromptu Speaking

One of the most frequently used methods of speech delivery is **Impromptu Speaking**. You'll begin to recognize this as speaking without prior preparation. Some call it "thinking on your feet." Impromptu Speaking is an ____________ way of communicating without having time to think of a clever answer or rehearsing what you might plan to say. It requires you to give a quick response at a moment's notice. This type of response is used in business meetings, job interviews, in the office, or anytime you are asked to speak without ____________________.

Use the **P.R.E.P. model** to **PREP**ARE anytime you deliver an impromptu speech:

Acronym	Stands for…	Description
P	Point	Restate question asked and clarify point of the question.
R	Relevance	Thank the person who asked the question, explain relevance, and provide a brief answer to the question.
E	Example	Provide a clear example as a follow-up to your answer and confirm an understanding of the answer.
P	Point	Summarize by restating the point and affirming that the question was answered.

Tips for Impromptu Speaking:
1. Anticipate impromptu speaking opportunities and be **PREP**ared.
2. Memorize the **PREP** model to be ready for anything.
3. Listen, so that you don't have to ask for the question to be repeated.
4. Don't rush! Take a moment to process the question before you begin to answer. Restating the question before you answer the point of the question will give you extra time to decide how to answer. The audience will think you are simply establishing good eye contact, when in reality, you are thinking of a clever answer. People who get in too big of a hurry are the very same people who will forget the question, ask for it to be repeated, and stumble over their answers. The biggest tip is to __________ ____________ ______________________.
5. The **PREP** model calls for ______________. Answers that get directly to the point of the question, connects the relevance of the question, and offers real-life examples affirms your credibility as a speaker.

Extemporaneous Speaking is used for prepared or formal speeches and in situations where you have ____________________ for searching topics, planning and conducting research, making visual aids, creating outline notes, and rehearsing the speech, but it is not memorized or written word-for-word. This type of speaking, which uses brief outline notes, gives the audience the impression that you are presenting the speech as it is created. This speech is ____________________ in nature and audiences tend to enjoy this type over others. Since there is rehearsal prior to the speech, the speaker can spend less time looking at notes and more time providing direct eye contact along with a more relaxed stage presence.

Tips for Extemporaneous Speaking:
1. Enthusiasm is contagious. Choose a topic you love.
2. Include personal stories and research to support the topic. Verbally cite research sources you use and explain how the research connects with the topic.
3. Create useful notes or use the app notes on your phone at the lectern. Keep notes simple and easy to use.
4. Rehearse a minimum of three times so you are familiar with the content, but do not memorize the speech. If you want to memorize something, only memorize the attention step, the title of the three main points, and the final comments.
5. Create effective and useful visual aids. Make sure you stay within the time frame allowed. Visual aids can objects or a PowerPoint presentation.
6. Pack everything you need and choose the outfit to wear the day *before* the presentation.
7. Arrive early to become familiar with the room, upload a copy of the PowerPoint (visual aid), set up displays, and stash a bottle of water near the lectern.
8. Greet attendees as they arrive so you can establish a connection with them prior to giving the speech.

Business Occasion Speeches are not very lengthy and usually get directly to the point, so they need to pack a punch. Words used during this type of speech need to be carefully chosen and precisely delivered to achieve the results you want. Work-related speeches include keynote addresses, welcome speeches, announcements, meetings, and reports.

Other **Business Occasion Speeches** might include **public relation addresses** designed to inform the audience about aspects to improve a problem such as attendance, insurance changes, policy, procedural adjustments, or changes in protocol. The speaker will need to establish goodwill and a positive atmosphere prior to delivering the required information. Additionally, the speaker should set a stage that will encourage the audience to accept the information being shared. Public relation speeches are not always met with approval; therefore, it is advisable to have the audience in your corner before delivering the information. Here is a brief explanation of other types of business occasion speeches:

____________________: This type of speech is presented at the beginning of a business event, meeting, or gathering. The person chosen to present this type of speech should use this as a point to welcome those in attendance. The **Welcome Speech** is a good time to introduce the agenda of the day, provide short announcements or reminders needed for the event, and to introduce the speakers on the agenda. Plan this speech to be welcoming, enthusiastic, light, short, and to the point.

Announcements: Regardless of the business or the organization, you can bet there will be announcements. The speaker should have a brief outline of notes, deliver an explanation of their purpose, and address the announcements in a speech that is short and to the point. Avoid leaving out pertinent information that would lead to the necessity of a second announcement.

Meetings and Reports: The purpose of conducting a meeting or presenting a report is to communicate information. This information may not be entertaining and usually involves details, numbers, charts, and data as a vehicle for information. Audience members appreciate effectively designed visual aids to see a visual report in the form of charts or graphs. The Speaker should be organized, keep visual aids simple, but include all necessary material for a complete report that is short and to the point.

Occasionally, you may be asked to offer the ___________ ___________ at a work event. If that is the case, consider it an honor usually reserved for established speakers. The first order of business will be to establish a connection or bond with the audience. Research the event, audience members, and organization sponsoring the event so your speech reflects the values, attitudes, beliefs, and behaviors of audience members. Understand the time restrictions for the speech so that you stay within the time allowed. Choose a topic that sets the tone for the meeting or conference and include the theme, if there is one.

Online meetings have become much more normal than in years past, so the next section will include things you need to know about conducting virtual meetings online along with best practices from the point of the host and the participants.

Virtual Meeting Platforms are applications and software designed so that we can meet remotely online. There are many different platforms, but they all seem to have a similar interface. The most common platforms are Zoom, Google Meet, Microsoft TEAMS, Skype, and Cisco WebEx, but you might also recognize other platforms as shown in the next slide.

Platforms may be presented for synchronous or asynchronous meetings as preferred by the user and the attendees.

_______________________ **meetings** are scheduled and happen through real-time interactions by phone, video conference, or in person. This type allows attendees to experience a more in-depth exchange and actively participate in the meeting. Not only will the speaker deliver content, but can involve the audience to brainstorm, address issues, invite feedback, or solve problems.

_______________________ **meetings** happen on your own time and are accessed through a recording, email, letters, texts, or direct messaging. Asynchronous meetings do not require everyone to be present at the same time. Depending upon the topic of the meeting, this type is often preferred because the attendee manages when the meeting starts, can pause the meeting to resume another time, and schedule a full review at a time that is best for the attendee.

Speakers who communicate clear expectations of virtual meeting room basics will experience less distractions and develop a positive environment so that audience members feel respected, included, focused, and engaged. Behaviors valued should be demonstrated throughout the meeting and formally established during the beginning of the virtual meeting transmission by the host.

Virtual Meeting Etiquette is an expectation of how meeting leaders and participants should behave during virtual meetings. Professional expectations for face-to-face meetings should also be observed during virtual meetings. This includes arriving on time, showing respect for others' ideas or questions, dressing appropriately, listening while someone else is talking, showing appreciation following a speech, and avoiding disruptive or distractive behaviors.

Tips for Effective Online Meetings:

1. **Find a quiet space** to join the virtual meeting without interruptions or distractions.
2. **Check your technology** to confirm the meeting platform you will need. Download any software prior to the meeting and be ready to begin on time. Check video and audio capabilities prior to the meeting.
3. **Check the lighting** in your meeting area.
4. **Mute the microphone and close the video camera until the meeting begins**. The speaker may mute all participants until after all content has been delivered. Be aware of any sights or sounds in your meeting area that can be seen or heard by attendees.
5. **Frame your face and shoulders** for a good camera view. Try to focus eye contact on the camera light and not on the window with your image or the image of others on the call.
6. **Be aware of the ______________ __________ and sounds** in your meeting space.
7. **Avoid eating or drinking** during virtual meetings.
8. **Dress, sit, act, and communicate professionally** as you would in a Face-to-Face meeting. Guard your facial expressions during the virtual meetings and be on your best behavior to NOT send the wrong message. Use the "Chat Box" responsibly.
9. **Sign in to the platform ten minutes prior to the start time**.
10. **Sign off and close the video window** after the meeting is over.

The host should always be _________________ and prepared for the meeting, start and end on time, and create a warm, inviting atmosphere where attendees feel comfortable.

Course Activity: Let's Talk About It!

How often are you involved in online meetings?

Are you usually the host or the participant in an online meeting?

When was your most recent online meeting?

What is your main "pet peave" when attending online meetings?

Do you prefer online meetings to Face-to-Face meetings?

Explain your response:

Do you have a prepared Elevator Pitch? You never know when you might happen to meet someone that could help you move up the corporate ladder. But imagine your disappointment, if you are so flustered by this chance meet-up that you can't think of the right words to say in such a short period of time. This is where the pitch comes in handy!

This is a short speech which allows you to __________ introduce yourself to someone in the time that it takes an elevator to move from one floor to the next. Even though this should be planned to follow the ________________ speech method, it should not sound rehearsed, but conversational. Always have an **Elevator Pitch** ready for job fairs, interviews, career expos, Facebook postings, LinkedIn, or for social events where someone might say, "Tell me about yourself!" If you don't already have one prepared, let's do this today.

Here is a brief outline of expectations for an Elevator Pitch.

Elevator Pitch

Use this short speech to quickly introduce yourself to someone during the time it takes to ride an elevator to the next floor.

- **Introduction:** begin with a greeting, handshake, name, job title, and personal tagline

- **Body:** explain why you chose this line of work, highlight experiences, strengths, show interest in listener, and present a business card

- **Closing:** ask for appropriate response for pitch, offer a handshake, and thank listener for time

Course Activity: Using the worksheet provided, plan and present a 2-minute elevator speech to introduce yourself and be prepared to use the Elevator Pitch Peer Review to evaluate the performance of your classmates.

Elevator Speech Planning and Brainstorming Guide:

    Introduction (one sentence)

        A.   Supply a greeting, your name, job title, and a personal tagline (examples below).

        B.   Extend your hand for a handshake or other acceptable form of contact (head nod, fist bump, wave).

  II. **Body (two or three sentences)**

        A.   Share why you chose this line of work and how it fits with your goals and values.

        B.   List top accomplishments and communicate what you have achieved that makes you proud, illustrate contributions you have made or problems you have solved.

        C.   Explain why people benefit from working with you.

        D.   Share strengths and experience: how you bring value or what you contribute to the organization.

        E.   Share the interest you have in the person to whom you are speaking.

        F.   Present a business card.

 III. **Closing**

        A.   Summarize what you hope to achieve from this brief meeting.

        B.   Thank the listener and let him know you appreciate his time.

        C.   Part with a handshake or other acceptable form of contact and an upbeat farewell greeting.

What is a personal tagline? This is not just a job title, but answers one or all the following questions: What do you do when you're doing your work? What is important about what you do? What change do you make for others? What do you do that is difficult to live without and worth paying for?

Example of a tagline:

- I am an accountant. I help people create a path for comfort and wealth.
- I am a Social Media expert. I build Facebook pages that help companies engage with their customers.
- I am an author and Professional Development Instructor. I help people become more prepared for the workplace.

Elevator Pitch Peer Review

Area	Excellent	Good	Fair	Not Observed
Introduction Sentence: Greeting Name Handshake Job Title Personal Tagline				
Body: Organized Pitch Clear Details Information Focused Effective Presented Business Card				
Conclusion: Restated Name Requested Response to Pitch Share Appreciation for Time Handshake Farewell Comment				
Delivery Skills: Vocal Skills Confidence/Enthusiasm/Smile Appearance, Poise, Posture Language Skills Gestures/Movement				

The purpose of an _______________________ is to coach, help, build, mold, and encourage. All of us can improve and leaders understand this concept. Evaluations of presentations allow speakers to recognize and capitalize on strengths to identify areas for improvement. By the same token, evaluations of job performance will allow employees to recognize strengths so they can identify weak areas for workforce development.

Using tools like the evaluation form we used for the Elevator Pitch is helpful for the speaker and for those listening to the evaluation. Evaluation forms are also created for workplace evaluation tools. Most organizations already have evaluation forms prepared and some require employee evaluations and self-evaluations as part of the process.

Tips for delivering feedback for speeches or work-task performances:
1. Create a performance file for each employee to track achievements.
2. Share _______________________ of the evaluation process.
3. Acknowledge employee successes and opportunities for improvement.
4. Review company and employee goals.
5. Be kind, but truthful and specific.
6. Define expectations for the job.
7. Create a mutually beneficial plan for _______________________opportunities.
8. Document expectations and progress.

As we cover best practices for becoming more effective communicators at work, we can't neglect **Socratic Leadership** as a proven method to stimulate ________ ________ and encourage a deeper commitment toward collaborating and exploring opportunities for improvement in the workplace. Leaders realize the importance of using effective listening and speaking skills daily, but did you know there is a method of speaking and ________ ________________that will challenge your peers and those in your departments to examine their own assumptions and knowledge? It is a simple, yet profound process.

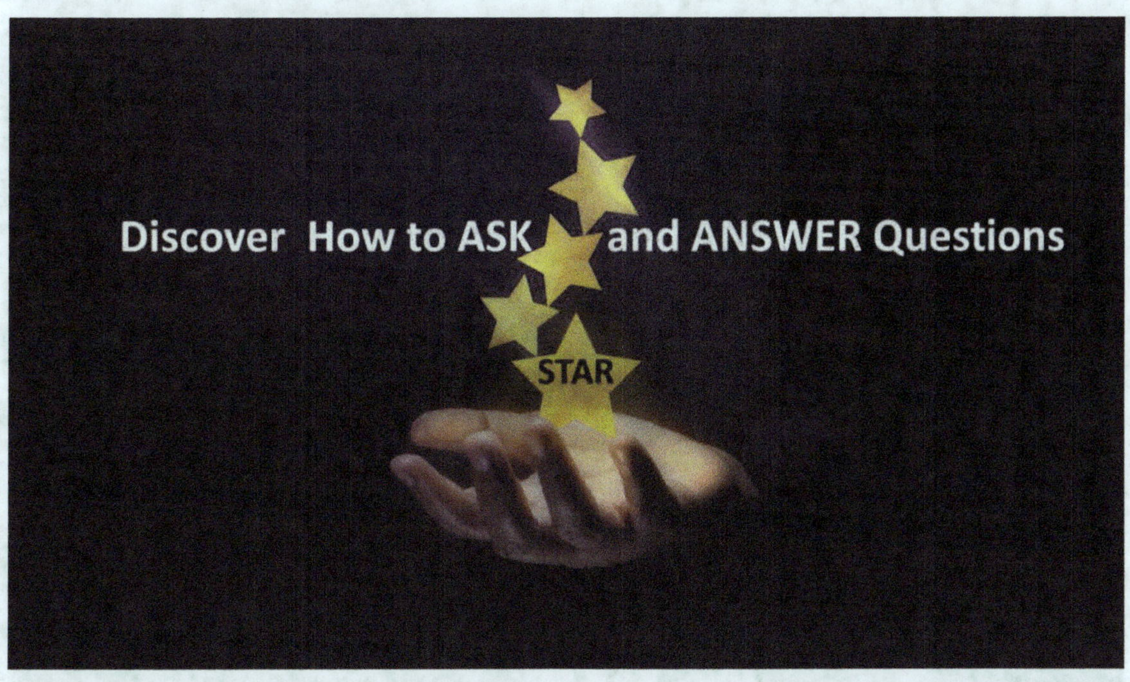

Course Activity: Test ideas and encourage each other to ask questions. There are three types of questions, but only one type actually motivates collaboration and teamwork. Can you identify and CIRCLE the question that would be best?

Leading Questions include an implied or explicit answer.
Closed Questions can be answered quickly with a yes or no and with little thought.
Open-ended Questions invoke thought and reflection, promote ideas, and uncover opinions and emotions.

Do you know how to ask an open-ended question? Write one in this area.

Click on the link to watch a video and see how the Socratic Method works (The Power of the Socratic Method): Bing Videos

Deciding HOW to ask a specific question can be challenging, so take a look at the **S.T.A.R.** model for creating open-ended questions that assess critical competences for discussion.

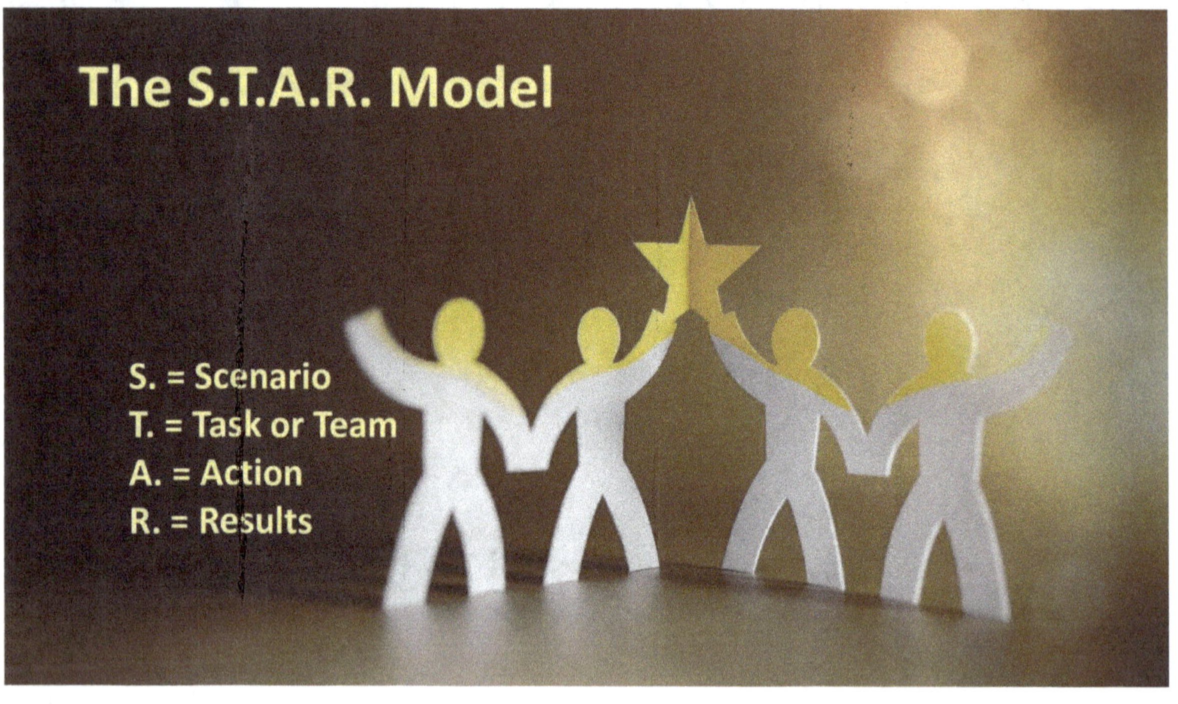

S = **Scenario:** Include a description of the ________________ or background of the event.

T = **Task or Team:** Include an option to involve collaboration to perform a task.

A = **Action:** Include a question that points to the __________ the applicant might take.

R = **Result:** Include a prompt for the applicant to share the outcome.

*Tip: Use **who, what, when, where,** and **why** words to motivate deeper answers.*

Here is an example of a good S.T.A.R. question:

(S) Imagine that you **(who)** are the leading manager of this company.

(T) We **(who)** are short staffed due to a flu breakout **(why)**, and your available team members are managing three times the normal daily workload **(what)**. There is a hard deadline **(when)** that our department must meet.

(A) *What* is the first thing you would say or do to prepare your employees for the deadline. *How* do you think your action would be received??

(R) *What* are the results or ______________ of meeting the deadline?

Now that you understand the formula for asking great questions, here are tips to help you accomplish **Socratic Leadership** like the boss that you are!

1. ______________: Avoid supplying all the answers. Instead, ask questions that help employees find the best answers by asking thought provoking questions.
2. **Be Humble**: Team members feel more inclined to openly answer questions if you don't ask the question with an ______________ but help them to find the answer.
3. **Engage, Rest, Recover:** Avoid asking too many questions or the employee may shut down. The ______________ helps engage others to answer the questions, but don't overdo the questioning process.
4. **Empower Others:** Not everyone will deliver the same answers and that is good because it allows for more perspectives______________ and ideas to surface. Encourage your team to be curious and find the best possible answer to meet the needs at hand.
5. **Question the possibilities, probabilities, and priorities:** Certain questions generate ______________while others test the outcome of the probabilities. This leaves us with the opportunity to prioritize and become aware of putting priorities in place for action.
6. **Improve Communication and Collaboration:** Explore solutions, collaboration, and ______________.

Participant Handbook Answer Key

Page: 4
- effective listening
- heard
- valued

Page: 5
- nonverbal
- respond
- confidence
- two-way interaction
- example
- honors
- respectful

Page: 7
- cues
- paralanguage
- eye contact

Page: 10
- interruptions
- preoccupations

Page: 11
- dialect
- response
- stress
- hierarchy
- appearance

Page: 12
- verbal
- senses

Page: 13
- hear
- thoughts
- perspective
- point

Page: 16
- Encoding
- Decoding
- Noise
- Feedback

Page: 17
- Voice
- influence

Page: 19
- body
- transition
- credibility

Page: 20
- credibility
- audience

Page: 21
- introduction
- three

Page: 23
- informal
- planning

Page: 24
- take your time
- brevity
- time
- conversational

Page: 26
- welcome
- keynote address

Page: 28
- synchronous
- asynchronous

Page: 29
- background view
- early

Page: 30
- quickly
- extemporaneous

Page: 33
- evaluation
- expectations
- growth

Page: 34
- critical thinking
- asking questions

Page: 36
- context
- action
- benefits

Page: 37
- goal
- ego
- scenario
- perspectives
- possibilities
- ideas

Video Links and Supplemental Materials

Bad Habit and the Cure: Present a scenario to the participants. Provide a good example and ask them to brainstorm a way to cure the problem.

- **Bad Habit Scenario:** Sometimes I may pretend to be listening, but my mind is on other things. **Example:** Last week my co-worker friend was telling me all about her weekend away with another set of friends. I'm sure the plans must have been fun for her, but my mind was on a work deadline that I had to meet by that afternoon. I was smiling, head nodding, and acting like I was listening to her, but in reality, I was stressing over how I was going to meet the deadline. When I actually focused back in on the conversation, she was asking me if I wanted to join her next weekend, but I had NO IDEA what she wanted me to join. How can I solve this problem?

Online Icebreaker Games: Use these to start a meeting and ask participants to post their response in the chat. This helps participants to become comfortable with posting messages and using the chat feature for the meeting, but you can also use the order of chat submissions as the order for speaking.

- **Phrases you might hear on a call:** Have participants post a laughing emoji in the chat everytime they hear one of the following phrases: Sorry, I was on mute! Can you hear me now? Could you repeat that? Who is speaking?

- **Host a background contest:** Choose a theme and ask participants to create a background. During the meeting, have the group choose a winner. The person who is the winner will share about their choice of background.

- **Pet Party:** Ask them to bring their pet to the meeting and let each person introduce their pet to the group. You can have folks vote on their favorite "Bring Your Pet to Work" entry.

- The Art of Listening by Simon Sinek **www.youtube.com/watch?v=qpnNsSyDw-g**
- How to be an Effective Listener and Why – Dr. Manny Steil
  www.youtube.com/watch?v=8Ze98hf5Gjl
- Try This the Next Time You Have an Uncomfortable Conversation by Simon Sinek
  www.youtube.com/watch?v=RcGkHrPSzDc
- How to be an Effective Listener and Why - Dr. Manny Steil
- How miscommunication happens and how to avoid it by Katherine Hampsten
  https://www.youtube.com/watchZv=gCfzeONu3Mo
- Any Successful Person MUST Do This! | Simon Sinek
- The Art of Active Listening by the Harvard Business Review Guide
  Bing Videos
- How to Use the Socratic Method for Dialogue, Debate, and Critical Thinking
  Bing Videos

Thank you for allowing me to join your journey towards leadership. It is my sincere desire to share helpful and realistic strategies with you. I'm your author, Dr. Penny Joyner Waddell, but most of my friends and colleagues call me the SpeechShark. That's because I serve as an author, professional speaker, speech coach, and seminar facilitator for local, state, national, and global industry leaders seeking to improve leadership and communication skills.

With a doctoral degree in Educational Leadership, an M.Ed in Instructional Technology Design with a concentration in Communication, and a B.A. degree in Speech Education along with experience gained through business, employment opportunities, and entrepreneurial endeavors, I have the background needed to facilitate professional development and continuing education seminars.

Designing, developing and presenting instructional content is a task which has provided lots of joy through the years. I'm the author of **Basic Writing for Business** and **Going from Stress to Success** (9th ed.) published by Pearson Publishers, **SpeechShark: a Public Speaking Guide** (4th ed.) and **CommunicationShark: a Human Communication Guide** (3rd ed.) published by Kendall Hunt, as well as the developer of the **SpeechShark** app designed to help people create, rehearse, and present speeches. Recently, I began working with Innovative Ink Publishers to produce facilitator and participant handbooks specifically designed for professional development seminar topics that enhance workforce readiness.

It was a supreme honor to receive the prestigious National Communication Association's Community College Educator of the Year Award, Georgia's Presidential Award from Toastmasters International, the Technical College System of Georgia's Rick Perkins Award for Excellence in Teaching from Gwinnett Technical College, and the coveted SkillsUSA National Educator of the Year Award for Career and Technical Colleges. While very much appreciated, these awards pale in comparison to the joy I feel when leading a seminar filled with industry leaders, managers, and staff members seeking enrichment to create a welcoming, professional, and enjoyable workplace.

For information or to book my services, please visit the website or contact me directly using the links below. I would also love to hear from you if you have suggestions of ways to make this a stronger course.

All my best,

Penny Joyner Waddell, EdD
www.SpeechShark.org
Penny@SpeechShark.org